MW01593379

The Wren's Cry

poems by Dorian Brooks

For Rhoda -

With all best wishes,

Dorian

Aug. '10

Ibbetson Street Press 2009

 *Published by:*

Ibbetson Street Press
25 School Street
Somerville, MA 02143

Copyright © 2009, by Dorian Brooks. All rights reserved.

Poems in this collection were originally printed in the following publications: *The Comstock Review, Goddessing Regenerated, Ibbetson Street, The Lake Street Review, Pegasus, Poetpourri, The Radcliffe Quarterly, River Wind, The Spring* (newsletter of the Rachel Carson Homestead Foundation).

Book design and cover photograph by Michael Alpert.

ISBN 978-0-9795313-5-4 / 0-9795313-5-7

For Pink

Contents

The Wren's Cry

Natural Order

Sometimes in summer
I imagine my grandfather
visiting his colonies of wild orchids
on Saltonstall Ridge.

His trips by motorboat
out to Faulkner's Island,
and the little girl who trailed her hand in the foam,
my mother.

He died when she was nine,
leaving behind his collection
of speckled eggs.

It's from him I inherit
my sense of the natural order
of things, and the flaming season
in which they happen.

All We Didn't Say

Spring Song

for my mother

Even as days lengthen,
you return
like April snow.

Woman I hardly knew,
in this soft time
I hear your voice
in the wren's cry.

Once we roamed spring
together, when you
taught me the words of morning.
Buds opened then
for us alone—
till something in the season
broke, and I turned
furiously from your side.

Years later I went to find you
along the old brook,
calling your name.
You'd become a petal
of shadow, borne
just beyond reach
on the swift wave.

Sponge Cake

Thumbing through my mother's
old recipe box, I find

frayed magazine clippings
and three-by-five cards

that tell in her fine hand
how she made those meals—

molded jello salad,
Sunday pot roast,

apple crumb pie.
But I can't find the one

for her sponge cake
she'd bake just for me

on my birthday. Then
I come to a card

pencilled with peculiar
squiggles and loops,

as if a small bird
had skittered across it.

Of course! It must be
her Gregg shorthand,

the script she used
when taking dictation

from busy men. So is this
her sponge cake recipe?

I could get a manual
and try to translate...

but I prefer the tang
of letting her keep

her secret, of simply
recalling the aroma

when the cake was done,
the lemon icing,

the candles, and the pleasure
we both felt as I lifted

the big silver fork
to cut the first piece.

The Soul as Butterfly

Past midnight, and the sleepers in this house
voyage outward.
I sit alone in the circle
of the lamp, remembering her—
mother, shy creature.

She was so quiet,
I could no more hold her
than water. Shock treatment
made her more withdrawn
than ever, a whitecap
on a far wave.

There are those to whom death comes
as a light wind
offshore. After the stroke
she sat for ten more years
gazing toward the horizon,
till at last her breathing
mingled into dawn.

All we didn't say
flutters about me now
in darkness.
And when I think
of her, though nothing
alights on my open palm,
I'm careful not to touch
those wings. And then I lose her
once more to air.

The Wish

for my father

Nights I close my eyes and you come to me
like a watercolor,
shirt pale as sky,
it's then I wonder, did we really stand
in a room with dusty curtains
and did you whisper: "Be strong.
The others have all betrayed me
or left. You're all I've got."

What that meant, how I lived with you
so long among boxes, scarcely breathing day,
till you'd finished revising despair's long manuscript
and I went to my honeymoon of regret.

And years later, when I boiled Cream of Wheat
for you stretched out on the sofa
dying, was I strong enough then, or could you tell
how my life and yours were pulling me apart
like a wishbone,
though you were the one who would break.

Did it matter that the tears
I gave up to earth
would not stay with you, running off in rivers
fuller than cello music but without sound.

Only on nights like this
does it come true, the wish
where I close my eyes and we're
sitting at a table somewhere
over beer,
not being strong at all but just
looking each other in the eye, talking.

On a Cold April Day

I get in my car
to do a quick errand.

Clouds sag overhead;
drops pelt my windshield.

I turn on the radio
to a Bach cello suite,

the one my father
used to play.

Chords reverberate
deep inside me

as I drive the music
across the rainy town.

In the rearview mirror
I glimpse the two of them

sitting in the back seat—
Johann Sebastian

in his curled wig, my father
with his unlit cigar—

chatting and laughing
like long-lost friends,

not paying the slightest
attention to me. I park

at a meter, then walk
along the wet street,

trying to etch the music
in my brain as bare trees

dance in the wind against
an unforgiving sky.

For My Father

I've come back to loving you
as surely as late apples in a bowl.
Since you died
nothing's quite the same, but still
the grass is cool in the night field
where once you taught me constellations.
When you said *Cassiopeia*
I memorized your voice,
larger than myth.

I've forgotten exactly when waves
started to whittle you down.
I was living in a different city
beyond music and laughter,
where the widest avenue was self-
knowledge and all the traffic streamed
away from fathers
toward a sky of blame.

Then in the audacity of your
dying, I took comfort
in bitterness, smothering you
with the white sheet of my indifference,
deadly as cancer. In this way
I shrank you to a small flame
in my hand. You went out
leaving no trace.

That was years ago. This morning
the acute light hurts
less than usual; at last I concede
the tenure of affection. And too
I see your photo on the bureau
as if for the first time—
father, man

turning in his own sorrow
silent as a planet,
who took my life with him
into darkness
and brings it back to me now
like a gift.

Waffles

On Sundays, supper was waffles.
Mother mixed the batter

in a big green bowl;
Father spooned it out

on an antique waffle iron.
With Jack Benny on the radio,

we dribbled maple syrup
over the crisp brown squares

before we ate. If, earlier,
our thoughts had been turned

to sin and redemption,
I've forgotten now.

What stays with me
are those Sunday evenings

when we sat at the kitchen table
leaning back in our chairs

just taking it easy,
for once not bickering

but joking and laughing
and telling stories—

lingering over our meal
as long as we liked,

passing the sticky plates
and asking for more—

living our own week's lesson,
partaking of the feast.

Myocardial Infarction

for my brother

How could the universe
so suddenly crack,
tearing the roots of childhood.

I think of you
ignoring dead weight
on your chest at midnight,
driving to work for days in pain,
then at last to the hospital.

And I wish I could reach in and
soothe red muscle as if
tenderness came naturally to us, and say
Poor tired thing,
poor wounded bird.

I want to find the old photo
of two kids laughing in winter—
you and me—and tell you
now more than ever
our lives are snowflakes
on our tongues.

Instead I call the main desk,
send a funny card.
Once you're out of danger
I dial direct:

the scarred fist of silence
opens in words that might just
heal us both.

Vista

Time can yield such clarity—
the way morning fog

disperses, revealing
shore birds and dunes.

And suddenly what we desire
has become as simple

as a white pebble,
smooth and round in the hand.

For so many years,
we followed a siren song:

position, wealth, advance—
all were part of the complicated

geography of attainment,
and none was enough.

Now we listen
for the low clang

of water and sky.
And we can live

in this modest light,
the color of sand.

In the Museum

In the natural history museum,
cranes and plovers
stand in their habitats
as if paralyzed.

I never loved you; nowhere
has it seemed more clear
than in this still corridor.

The night you announced,
"I want to marry you,"
I entered a landscape
frozen behind glass.

Love was an unknown species
then. And it took me
years to discover
how skilled you were
in the precise taxidermy
of the heart.

We were so lifelike,
somehow retaining
all our natural colors
even in stasis.

Finally, inch by inch,
I started moving
toward that barely perceptible seam
where space merges
into a painted background

of grasses and a distant
trail of extinct bison
winding across a prairie
under an open sky.

Willows

Salix babylonica

How beautiful they are
in their sadness, pale gold
against the smoke-brown hills
of early spring.

While we're out walking,
you're planning a visit
to the west coast, eager
for new places, though
knowing I can't go with you.
And I turn in silence
to the willows and their soft
rain of light.

Timeless, they touch
the depths of loss.
I imagine them
along a riverbank,
lithe as dancers
mourning whole kingdoms
in the slight swaying
of wrists and tresses,
the lamentations of air.

We continue our walk,
you chatting about your trip
while I harbor sorrow
on my own shore,
among my own kind.

Now Summer

Now summer, soft madrigal
we'd almost forgotten, returns.

Soon I'll be wearing my light
cottons and you'll be looking

all over for screen doors.
Remember the long novels

we used to read aloud
to each other, in the old

garden—*The Moonstone,*
The Woman in White?

Bees hummed by the trellis,
the air sweet with petals

scattering around us.
But somehow, those hours

gave way to shadow.
We need to go back

to lightness, back to
the tea rose of first acquaintance.

Whether it's your voice
pausing over the sleepwalker as he

steals the gem, or mine
stunned by the hooded face of

madness that turns out to be
sane as morning,

we'll let the stories
hold us once more

as a mild wind
listens in the maple trees

and days lift like pages
over the grass

where we lie.

Reunion at Point Odiorne

for Muriel and Bill

At the seaside park
we balance the afternoon
on our fingertips, the sky
clear as blown glass.

Cries of children and gulls
swirl like memory,
the tide surging
to pools of weed and crab.

How long has it been, we say,
watching the slow waves
gather, lift
and break on the rocky shore.

How can we hold this day
like the white sloop passing,
whose sails shimmer forever
out on the endless blue.

The Earth I Travel On

Back Road

If there's time, I'll drive to work
on a back road, past pale fields

shadowed with willows and oaks
and a river holding the stillness

of morning sky. I'll plan my day
to a heron I see on the marsh,

then slow on a curve for a sudden
scurry of fur. I want to stop

and run my hand over the round
earth I travel on and call it holy

in the burnished light. I want to wake
to the pure fire of being

alive on a back road,
driving to work.

At Martha's Point

On a day in early spring,
sick of the city, we drive out
to the edge of the woods.

We pull briars aside
to follow a path
through stands of pines,
past fallen logs
and old stone walls,
then stop on a cliff
at a point of land
overlooking the river.

Beneath a lone cedar
we sit for a while,
letting the sunlight
warm us, gazing
where river currents
carry the pale sky
far as the horizon,
a rose-gray haze of trees.

Somewhere in the silence
a blackbird calls; once
we hear below us
the lilt of voices
from a passing canoe
trail off into distance.

In this place
of light and water
and weathered rock
silver with lichen,
the ground presses
its brittle filigree

of dead leaves and twigs
into our bodies.
So this is home.
I breathe deep,
wondering at how long
we've been away.

Cricket

after Rachel Carson

Just at dusk,
from tall grass
comes a rhythmic
whisper. I know
it's *Oecanthus
niveus*; but

who is he,
shy musician
with his soft
syllables? I
move a bit

closer, causing
silence—until
he rims the night
again in silvery

song. Crouched
low, I hold my
breath as if

I might catch
his meaning—

listen listen

Ground Zero

for David

On November 6, 1971, the U.S. carried out
its largest underground nuclear test ever,
on Amchitka Island in the Aleutians.

Learning of the explosion
only now, 25 years later,
I look back on that date
and think of you, born
two days before.

At first, everything
seemed normal; but
as your breathing slowed
and doctors frowned,
I saw your life become
a wisp of hours—
pale blue beads
in the ID bracelet
on your wrist.

Updates on your condition
eclipsed all other news.
For a while, I ignored
your faltering pulse,
dreaming we might flee
from probing instruments
to someplace safe—
maybe a mossy island
sheltered from the waves,
where eagles rode the wind
and curlews sang...
till I saw in a flash
the coming storm:
I held you
one last time,

and then I let a nurse
wheel you away.

I remember how doctors
huddled, lacking answers.
Now, reading about Amchitka,
I learn of sea otters
found with eyeballs driven
deep into their skulls
by the force of the blast,
and nuclear debris
leaking into creeks and rivers
ever since

and I can't help thinking,
No wonder you left.

Pollution

How lovely the white froth is
floating downriver,
as if it had nothing to do with death,
but were merely the sky's lace hem.

May we all know something of beauty
as breath goes out from us:
fish, choked with chemicals,
dream they fall in a rain of gold,
and gaunt men and women
waver down on ash wings
into silt, and the memory of elms.

August

By late summer, the maples
have gathered so much darkness
among their boughs,
we finally concede
our own maturing.

We hear crickets and mourn
an earlier music,
the days grown shorter now,
even our few words
a measure of acquiescence.

And in time,
longing itself dwindles
to a single leaf—
fine-veined and lucent,
yet trifling.

Day closes
and we are one
with the vesper sparrow,
at home with solitude
and night descending.

Toadflax

Maybe in another life
I'll come back as a weed—

a blue toadflax,
standing by the roadside

parallel with my fellows,
holding a pale flower

to the sun.
And I'll remember

this life—
how often I whizzed past

the little things,
looking back on them

too late,
a wavering

comb of moments
behind me.

Wetlands

summer 2007

In the fifth year of the war,
I take an afternoon off

and drive to the wetlands
near the Missouri River.

A dirt road winds among
tall grasses and trees;

low clouds are mirrored
in a maze of shallow creeks

where, on half-sunk logs,
turtles bask in the pale sun

and blue herons stand
motionless, as if

in a Chinese painting.
Breathing such quiet air,

I almost forget the war.
Turning to leave, I notice

a lone bare tree, its limbs
holding a flock of egrets

like so many white candles,
or souls of the newly dead

pausing a moment
in this place of stasis—

stunned, as if wondering
what they died for.

Green Man

Ancient spirit,
you're as far from us

as those forgotten woods
where deer and salmon leapt.

Still, we may see your face
inside an old church—

carved on the rood screen
or high above the nave—

oak leaves flowing
from your head, flowing

from your mouth as if
you spoke the world alive.

Now in the stained glass light
we linger, wondering...

If we could touch
your lips we might hear

your voice, intoning
the lost word for home.

October

Now by yellow leaf-light
we come once again
to this turning,

as dreams age
and days glide downward
on a crow's wing.

Afternoon shadows
gather low
over the fields,

moving like women
among the last
bright gleanings.

A pine cone thuds:
something in the sound
makes us want to hold

what we have—
a love,
a thin moon.

And we pause,
listening for echoes
old as memory,

husking our lives
to the core,
the dark bonfire.

A Sudden Darkness

David

November 4–8, 1971

When you came down that slow canal
into light,
you thought it was the wrong country—
France, maybe, the Seine—
and never even waved to us,
but kept on going till you disappeared
under a far bridge.

What difficulty we had then
with language,
saying *chromosomes*
and holding the word close like a replica
of you, or the brief glimpse
you'd given us:
brown hair,
mouth curved in the trajectory
of a summer star.

What could we do but roam the narrow streets,
as if the light rain
falling and falling around our eyes
would let us remember you
in the way the mist
never quite lifted
from rooftops and spires.

Little prince,
when I sit in the park these days
on my lunch hour,
dark birds
swarm at my feet.
I open a paper bag and break
bread in your name.

Blue Spruce

"All my relations"

Glancing out at the sky
this wintry afternoon
as darkness gathers early

like an old acquaintance
at my window, I think:
if we are all kin,

then I may be cousin
to the blue spruce towering
next door. A sudden

commotion in the street
draws me outside to see
two men emerge from

the house next door, carrying
a bagged form on a stretcher
into a waiting hearse.

"Suicide," says one.
"The woman in the top apartment.
Three weeks ago. Nobody

found her till today."
Doors slam; engines start,
and I'm left asking others

who she was. "Wasn't she young?"
a neighbor ventures. "Blonde?"
Another adds, "I'm pretty sure

her name was Cynthia."
I can't place her at all.
I'm left wondering

how people can live
so close together
and never meet, their days

tumbling past each other
without touching.
Cynthia, moon woman,

I stare now at your window
high in the spruce's shadow,
imagining your mail

piling up on the stairs
like so many shells
on an abandoned shore.

Deer

In the kitchen at 4 a.m.
you set down your bags
and slump into a chair.
"I'm just tired from the trip,"
you sigh—
but your worn face
worries me.

Shuffling to the sofa,
you say you drove all night
just to get home.
Somewhere in Pennsylvania
the pain began,
high in your chest,
bad enough to make you
stop at a rest area.
After that, you saw
dim shapes in the darkness
all along the roadside—deer
come down from the mountains
to feed in the tall grass.
They moved in twos and threes,
maybe twenty in all,
not scared, not even looking up
as you drove past.

Now, waiting beside you
for the doctor to call back,
I see them too.
As you turn in sleep,
they draw nearer.
In the shadows
they nuzzle and browse,
dipping their heads

so close I can almost
feel them breathe...

if only they'll stay
till morning

Absence

High in Asian mountains,
when someone takes a trip
a shaman has to free the soul for travel—
pig shriek and incantations
over blood and carcass.

For you in D.C.,
it took something more
to set you wandering:
your son, seventeen
racing the Mustang
around the test lot
out of control, then
smash
and he was gone.
By the time I heard the news,
you'd left your dazed family
for Canada, alone.

And I want to say I know what there is
about remote cafés
that holds such broken light—
nothing that can heal, but simply
a sense of yourself staring into a candle
in an endless country, charting
the bones of your own hand.
As though even memory were a journey,
a matter of spanning the distance
between his first-born cry
and where you sit now,
without tears or photos,
wondering which way to go.
Any village will do—
river or spire, a language
you don't understand.

Farthest away is the thought
of going home; but finally
the road curves back
and you follow.
Someone has cleared out
his room, disposed of his things.
Only absence remains,
that white peak
from which he can never fall,
nor you descend.

Titanic

for Jim White

Watching an old movie about the Titanic
for the fourth time,
hoping somehow it'll turn out differently:
another ship will see the distress rockets
and rescue everyone.

Deluding myself as usual.
Like that time in the restaurant,
you with only months to live,
complaining how none of your friends would accept it—
none but me.
You ordered a salt-free lunch,
then stared down at your plate and thanked me
for my honesty.
For not saying,
"My uncle Fred had the same condition
and lived to be ninety."

But I too ignored what loomed
massive as ice: never admitting
my blind panic,
my prayer exploding in the night sky.

The truth is always best,
that was the fiction you asked of me
when we'd get together for errands or coffee
that final spring.
I gave you a version
brave as any hymn,
closing my ears to the long roar
of you being gone.

Radium Girl

Katherine Schaub was one of hundreds of young women who worked at the U.S. Radium Corporation in Orange, New Jersey, in the early 20th century, painting numerals on wristwatch and instrument dials with luminous paint. Many of the women became ill, some fatally. Schaub died in 1933 at age 31.

1. 1917–1921

I was 15 when the company
hired me. How I loved my job!
It was tricky at first,
shaping the tiny numerals
just right; but I soon caught on.
I'd moisten my brush with my lips
to give it a fine point,
as the foreman taught us.
And we had such fun!
When we turned off the lights,
we saw radium glowing
everywhere—on our clothes
and hair and skin. Some girls
even painted their teeth
to surprise their boyfriends.
Plus—as the company told us—
we were helping the war effort.
I was so proud.

*They never told us
what radium does
inside the body,
nor that its half-life
is 2,000 years.*

2. 1922–1927

A year after I left,
my jaw went bad.
The pain was unbearable.
I had two teeth removed,
but got no relief.
Others too came down
with peculiar symptoms—
like my cousin Irene,
one of the first to die.
Not for several years
did doctors say it was radium
that made us sick, although
we had our suspicions.
The company said the cause
was our own poor hygiene,
and tried to block a lawsuit.

I might have given way
to tears, but I knew
they wouldn't help.

3. 1928

At last, a settlement!
My hip hurt so, I could hardly
climb the stairs to the courtroom,
but they gave five of us
$10,000 each!
Then the doctors gave us
a year to live; so I thought,
okay—for a year I'll be
Cinderella at the ball.
After I pay my debts,
I'll buy some pretty clothes,
stay at a country resort
and try horseback riding—
maybe even get a car!

*I loved to sit on the porch
and gaze at the hollyhocks.
With lots of fresh air and sunshine,
I began to think—after all,
why shouldn't I get well?*

4. 1929–1930

Relapse. Months in the hospital.
Anemia. Radium necrosis.
Terrible pain in my knee.
A fall; a fracture; an X-ray—
cancer of the bone.

I'm so tired of this experiment.

5. 1931–

I can walk again,
if I use my brace and cane.
It's really my faith in God
that keeps me going.
I don't want any more treatment.
What I want most of all
is to write—to help others
by telling my story.
That, to me, is happiness.
If only I live long enough!
But even now, I'm blessed:
I close my eyes and
I see God's face—

radiant
timeless

Chemotherapy

We who have wild
cells lurking
in our systems
come here for treatment.
Nurses in lab coats
dispense their potions
through plastic tubing
into our veins,
calming our fears
of nausea and hair loss.

They ask how we feel;
some of us grieve
for the parts of
our bodies lost
to the surgeon's knife.
And we tend to brood
on the future,
that slow river
that once meandered
to distant mist,
where now a sudden
darkness could fall.

As for our daily
lives, there are words
we can taste
like never before:
*Husband. Child.
Star. Morning.*
Passing waste places,
our eyes gather
the drabbest weeds
like lilies, like love.
Look! We exclaim

at the clinic window,
pointing out the strange new
halo of fire
around everything.

Fantasy

"Living erotically is being alive."
                    –Hallie Iglehart Austen

At dinner you mention
a book of sex fantasies.
I toy with my calzone

and mumble an expression
of interest. The truth is,
when I'm with you

I hear another kind
of heavy breathing—words
we've carried for two years:

in your case, the medic
who leaned and said,
You're having a heart attack;

in mine, the surgeon's
voice on the phone:
Bad news. It's a tumor.

So here's my fantasy:
we'll meet at this table
overlooking the river

ten years from now,
swapping duck puns
and weaving a narrative

from the intimacy
of evening light
and silence

as the waiter lifts his eyebrows
to see us so fantastically
alive, our skin singing.

Breast Cancer Dream

She dreams of trees
along a city street,

branches cut away
to make great gaps

so electric power lines
can pass. Maimed

though they are, the trees
live on. *Dance with us!*

they call. She steps out
and takes the leafy arm

of a lopsided maple;
and as they sashay

up and down the avenue,
their empty places

touching, she feels
whole again—as if

she and the trees might keep on
dancing all night, as if

nothing has ever
gone wrong.

Swimming With the Dolphins

(photo, Boston Globe, spring 1987)

The girl who is thin and bald from cancer
is swimming with the dolphins
in Florida. This is her last wish.
In two days she will die, but now
she and her father and the dolphins
are bobbing and diving together
laughing,
loving the water and the cool motion
of their legs and flippers.

The father has traveled
over and over among the fifteen years
of her life—white archipelago
tapering to sky,
the spot on the X-ray
the one black sail.
He has hammered his heart
into a boat, and he keeps it hidden
in the pebbled cove of his composure.

She will tire soon;
and when he lifts her and they say
good-bye to their new friends,
she will have that lightness
the body takes on after attaining
the one pure arc.
                    When he lowers her
she will be so light—as if
she were no longer substance
but song; and he will hear it
as he punts the craft
offshore,
          he will hear it
as he lets her go
over the waves.

Who She Was

Word of Mouth

"Writing was a form of death."

—*A.S. Byatt,* Possession

Was it the wind
who first told stories
long ago, or was it

a mother murmuring
"Once upon a time"—
her child dreaming,

beyond the hearth,
a moonlit forest
and beckoning path.

Whoever spoke,
that voice echoed
through the centuries

in royal castles
and roadside inns,
a voice giving shape

to talking foxes,
ogres, Ash Girl.
Memory's breath

danced in the telling—
every tale a nimble
pirouette, with never

the same words twice.
How alive they were,
always evolving in air.

How still they are,
fixed in print
on the white page.

To Brigit

Brigit is the ancient Celtic Goddess of healing, smithcraft and poetry, associated with fire and sacred wells.

In the harsh
metallic winter,
when I tried to sing
my tongue stuck
in ashen air
my voice died

When I tried to breathe
my heart stalled

Cold mists
corroded my sleep

Now you come
rinsing the land
in buttery light,
touching the willows
with your wand

My body
stirs

I wake to the cry
of new-born lambs

My song
flares in your footsteps
like windflowers

Brigit
I am water
swirled in a dish
to catch your eye

Dance with me

I am the Earth
opening
to your fire

Hold me
Heal me

Sagging Breasts: What to Do?

Love them. Let the moon
caress them as perhaps

she has not done
for decades. If milk

flowed in them, let fingers
trace a moon-blue memory

of love. Let them whisper
their softnesses to silk

or cotton—they are natural
as autumn. Let them droop

and sway in the warm curves
of a woman's story,

whatever lies are spoken
in their name.

May

"the merry month of May"

I'm in love with May—
with maple trees tossing
pale chartreuse tassels
against a gray-gold sky,
and at the lawn's edge,
clusters of bluets'
tiny white stars.

Give me a mossy bank
by a stream, and a book
of old tales of spring—
Maypole dances
and midnight bonfires,
people rising at dawn
to hear the cuckoo sing.
Tales of housewives
who lured swarming bees
with lemon balm and thyme
to build hives nearby,
then talked to them as friends;
tales of wise women
who gathered cowslips
and elderflowers for healing,
who set out bowls of milk
after dark, for the fairies.

In this magic season,
I want my life to unscroll
with fiddlehead ferns,
gathering its story
from earth, rain and sun.
I long to learn the ways
of wild dogwood buds
as they open—

floating over the forest
as in a dream,
wafers of light
in the soft air.

Hypatia

Hypatia was an Alexandrian mathematician and philosopher.
In 415 A.D. she was brutally murdered by a group of monks.

They flensed my body clean
as bone. Who can blame them?
After all, I stood for
reason in an age of
piety so great,
the sky still glowed
from the library's burning.
I read Plato and pondered
the distances of stars,
my mathematics intricate
as lace. Double offense:
a woman with a mind.

You understand, I was doomed.
When I saw the monks thronging
toward me, I knew my fate.
If any of them faltered
before he dipped his shell—
honed edge gleaming—
beneath my white robe
to gouge my flesh away,
it was only a moment
until his vision claimed him
once more: centuries
of darkness, with intellect
shorn thin as ribs
singing only of God, His Word
against mine.

Lammas

for Professor Emanuel Rudolph

Lammas is the old Celtic festival of the early grain harvest,
celebrated on August 2.

At first harvest,
as women heap the altars

with fruits and grains, I come
bearing your death. I offer

the story: you stopped
at the sign but didn't see

the other car speeding toward you
on a country highway.

Removed by air-lift,
you clung to life

for three days, then
fell to stillness.

Your colleague wrote the news
to friends. I devoured

details of your career
I'd never known—your expertise

in lichens of Antarctica,
the glacier that bears your name.

I recalled how kind and funny
you were, and your love

for old botanic lore
and stories for children.

Dear Professor,
the year ripens, even

in your absence.
I mourn you

as the dark earth yields
its shimmering tassels,

marking the season's
wild appetite.

Historical Marker

Imagine finding—maybe
in a tangled grove
where larch and crabapple

thin the summer sun—
an old granite slab
chiseled with these words:

"On this site, no man
was ever bayoneted
or shot, no battle

fought for God or country.
But once, long ago
a woman lay here

gasping and straining
while another gripped her hand
and wiped her brow

for hours, then lifted
her baby to her breast.
And as the evening light

touched their tired faces,
the moss glistened crimson
on this unscarred ground."

Samhain

*Samhain (October 31) is the ancient Celtic festival
of the beginning of winter and the new year,
a time to remember the ancestors.*

At the dying time of year,
when we are closest
to your world,

remember us
as streams remember
oaks. Grieve

lightly—let the landscape
hold your sorrow,
the way pale ferns

along a stone wall, part
in bursts of asters.
We need so little,

moving from mist
to shadow.
It is enough

that you dream us
back from the dark
by candle-flame,

our names a whisper
on your lips. Then
we can continue

on our way, knowing
we are with you still
in the glint of frost

on sumac, the cries
of geese arrowing south
over the burning fields.

In Memoriam

University of Montreal Engineering School
December 6, 1989

I keep thinking about his smile
and whether the women saw it
when he entered the classroom

Geneviève Hélène Nathalie Barbara Anne-Marie

When he ordered the men to leave
and lifted his rifle
did the women think,
Well he's smiling so maybe he really
means no harm

Maud Barbara Maryse Maryse Anne-Marie

Then with each quick shot
hitting its mark
like exploding roses,
did he smile some more
Was he that little boy charmer
knocking over the dolls
stealing the candy

Sonia Michele Annie Annie (the woman he missed)

And at the end
when he tossed his life away
after theirs,
did his smile die too
or does it still hang in the empty classroom
near the chalk dust and the erasers
like a curve with no equation
like a mathematical expression
for love

80

Sea Child

after Nuala Ni Dhomhnaill

In an old tale, a woman
is swimming one day
in the sea, when

she feels a sort of shadow
weaving around her body
underwater. Her skin

grows scaly and her eyes
pearl-like as she descends,
lured by the sunless depths

till all at once she turns,
swims back to the surface
and hurries to the shore

and to her husband.
Nine months later,
she gives birth to a boy

with seaweed and shells
in his hair. His eyes
are big and round and blue

and never close,
but seem always fixed
on some distant mist...

I wonder if the tale
came from a mother's dream
as she held her child, born

with stunted limbs and vacant
eyes, who never slept,
his cry as haunting

as a seal's. I like to think
she took some comfort
from the tale—a skein

of dreamlight circling
around her and her child,
carrying them back

down watery depths
to that first cradle
where life began,

their lullaby a shadowy
silence, the two of them
together, whole.

Who She Was

Perhaps a woman
sat in her kitchen late at night
writing, while a candle
burned low.

There may have been no sound
but now and then a murmur
out of some deep dream,
and the quiet scratching
of her pen:

Dear Abiah,
I have gathered fresh herbs
near the woods' edge at midsummer
for this poultice—comfrey, yarrow
and elecampane...

If a cry
made her rush to tend a fever
or calm a fright,
she came back
and resumed:

I love pennyroyal
best of all,
growing in the back field
like tufts of sky.
Here is the recipe
for my good tea...

Then if she drowsed
and if the curtains
parted, a night wind
lifting the pages upward

light as ash
beyond the moon,

perhaps they fell

in a daughter's drawer or in another
century where someone
smoothed the yellow corners
and just made out the hand, saying

I wonder who
wrote this. I wonder
who she was.

Snow on Water

Except Nebraska

On tv they're selling
gadgets galore,
the offer good anywhere—
except Nebraska.

Such things aren't needed there.
The people are special;
they're who we are
on the other side of the mirror,
at night roaming the blue fields
of our childhood,
dreaming of horses
on our behalf.

Even their language is different.
Where we say *hurry*,
they trace a swallow's arc;
they say *loneliness*
the way smoke rises
from someone's chimney.
And when they lie down
in summer grass,
then they're silent,
letting the wind
praise the wide sky.

Nothing more is known about them.

Whales

On New Year's Day the zoo
is free, so I join the throngs
to watch the Beluga whales.
As their huge white bodies
arch and descend
in watery light,
I want to cry with them
all the way to the bottom
of what I've longed to say
in my own dying language.

How, as the year begins,
we stand poised like skiers
with the wide glade of morning
before us,
under a sky so blue
the merest stray leaf
could spill the universe.

If only we had the right instinct
to tell us what to do,
we could get on with our lives
without this dread—like wearing
a necklace of tiny bells,
one for each task:
Listen.
Echo laughter.
Study the history
of moonlight on bare stone.

Through the deep viewing window,
these great ocean creatures
frolic and drift.
Whatever it means
to be human, it can slip

through our grasp like a cheap toy—
the way we toss grave-flowers
from a safe distance, denying
our own part in closing
the meek lids of the dead.
And should our worst fear
happen, shall we then blame
the winds that scatter us
in endless night?

More and more people crowd in
out of the cold to stare
at the glad whales, then slowly
we twist along a hallway
upward past tropical fish
into daylight. From here
we look back on the pool's
unbroken surface with only
the thin harpoon of remembrance,
and a sense that the heart
is an open book where
nothing is written except
whom we shall love, whom not,
snow on water.

Friendly Fire

I wonder if
a victim of

friendly fire
is any less

dead—is dying
like a dream?

Perhaps when fire's
friendly, the body

stirs slightly in
the flag-draped dark

as if to rise
and say, "Hold it!

Who're ya firin' at?"
before *Taps* sounds.

And I think the woman
whose hand touches

the photo in its
polished frame

and then covers
her face, must know

he can't really be
gone—so friendly

do his boots look
under his bed.

Loon

Tuning in the news
on my car radio, I hear

the same old stories—armies
slaughtering each other

for peace, corporations
counseling the poor

for profit. So I switch
to a tape—"The Cry of the Loon,"

and I'm back in the ramshackle
cabin we had by the lake

last summer. Waves lap
under the porch as breezes

fray curtains to mist
at nightfall, a pale moon

rising over the water
where darkness holds

the world in silence
and wild laughter.

How Our Dead Come Back To Us

for W.

They come back by night,
airborne over the ocean
to touch down in darkness
on our eastern shore.

We never see them arriving,
casket by casket. It is forbidden
to witness their terrible silence,
their flag-bright shrouds.

But we know they keep coming,
body by fallen body.
And as they come, we hear
waves thundering like drums—

    for what   for what   for what
    for greed   for lies   for nothing.

Bain-Marie

The invention of the double-boiler, or bain-marie,
is attributed to an alchemist named Mary.

To think it was invented
by a woman—

this way of tempering heat
and using it

to clarify and soften,
without a trace

of charred pot
or smoking ruin.

Flight

Shamans in Siberia were considered hostile
to the Soviet regime; many were dropped
out of airplanes and challenged to fly.

My only hope
is that in fact
they did fly,

spirits soaring
light as drumsong
to the upper world

as bodies plunged
to hit stony ground
or metal sea.

Surely they did fly—
the way a poem
born of shadows

can lift off
to the sun,
leaving behind

the dull thud
of everyday life,
the dead heart.

Tumbleweeds

Tumbleweeds thrive wherever
land use has disturbed the soil.

As a child, roaming
Connecticut hills,
I dreamed of being

a cowgirl; and lo—
on my tenth birthday
I was one! I had

a pair of silver pistols,
big hat, fringed skirt.
I rode an old sawhorse

into the sunset, shooting
Indians, singing the words
to "Tumbling Tumbleweeds":

I'll keep rolling along
Deep in my heart is a song
Here on the range I belong

while all around me,
shadows of other words
were drifting over the land—

Pomperaug   Hammonasset
Quinnipiac   Naugatuck
Mohegan   Connecticut

Why didn't I hear them?

Mariposa

Spanish for butterfly.
I love the way the sound

lifts so lightly in air.
How odd to read

that, in old California,
it was also the name

of the U.S. battalion
sent to fight the Indians

who lived in what became
Yosemite National Park.

Mariposa. I can't get
the sound out of my head

as I stare at the famed
black and white photo

of the park's great Half Dome,
pale moon rising over

sheer rock, no living thing
in sight. Maybe the souls

of the dead really do
come back as butterflies—

or else maybe as words
that, when spoken, flutter

across time, on wings
brighter than blood.

The Conquering People

I am one of
the conquering people
who claimed this land
long ago
Centuries later
I hover still—
lonely, aloof
alien in air

I might have lived
with partridge and deer
in the dense forest,
but wilderness
held such terror
I had to destroy
what I could not love

I heard night's
soft moccasin
and shot to kill
I carved sunrise
into coins
I strode and glittered,
an iron giant
paving the seasons
in molten stone

O wind flute
O lost prayer
of lake and eagle
help me
I fall like ash
How many times
must I die
by my own
conquering hand

Stones

Approaching the site
in the gathering dusk, I see
what look like strands of pearls—
rows and rows of white stones,
hundreds in all, one
for each child who died here.

This is the Indian cemetery
at Carlisle, Pennsylvania's
Army War College,
once a boarding school.
The founder, Colonel Pratt
of Civil War glory,
proclaimed his goal:
"Kill the Indian, save the man."
For forty years, children
were brought here from tribes
all over the continent
to live by Army rules,
forced to give up
their long hair and names.
Those who still dared
speak their native tongue
were sent to a stone dungeon.

Some got an education,
then went home too changed
to fit back in; others
never left this place,
but died of disease
or loneliness
or a broken heart.

I pause by a stone inscribed
"Tabitha Carroll, Arapaho,

Feb. 18, 1893."
In the grass, someone has left
three small cloth horses.
They seem to be running
as if eager to flee,
carrying the girl's spirit
with them. And I almost
envy her—riding with the wind,
free of this land's
bloody history
and heavy stones.

Monarch

for Kevin Pourier

Monarch butterflies are threatened by genetically engineered
corn and by logging of their over-wintering sites in Mexico.

In an old photograph
of the great Lakota leader

Sitting Bull, he's wearing
a hat with a wide brim

and in its band,
a monarch butterfly.

This was around the time
Sitting Bull was suspected

of promoting the Ghost Dance
and was arrested

by police who then
shot him dead,

as, two weeks later
at Wounded Knee, soldiers

shot dead some three hundred
Lakota people.

No one knows how the monarch
got on Sitting Bull's hat—

if he put it there,
or if it alighted

on its own.
Maybe the monarch

felt itself kin
to the holy man

and wanted to be with him
for a while.

Maybe they both knew
what was coming.

Dorian Brooks is a retired technical writer and a researcher in women's history. Her poems have appeared in numerous magazines and anthologies and in the book length collection *A Pause in the Light*. She is an assistant editor for *Ibbetson Street* magazine.